THE POWER OF INTERCESSION

STUDY GUIDE

ISBNs:

ISBN: 978-3-944924-22-9 (softcover)

ISBN: 978-3-944924-10-6 (eBook)

Bible Versions:

NKJV: All scripture quotations, unless otherwise indicated, are taken from the New King James Version ®. Copyright © 1982 by Thomas Nelson, Inc. Used by permission. All rights reserved.

AMP: "Scripture quotations are taken from the Amplified ®Bible, Copyright © 1954, 1958, 1962, 1964, 1965, 1987 by The Lockman Foundation Used by permission." (www.Lockman.org)

THE MESSAGE: "Scripture taken from The Message. Copyright © 1993, 1994, 1995, 1996, 2000, 2001, 2002. Used by permission of NavPress.

Word Definitions:

Taken from: Nelson's Illustrated Bible Dictionary, Copyright © 1986, Thomas Nelson Publishers Vine's Complete Expository Dictionary of Old and New Testament by Thomas Nelson 1996

First printing: 2007 - Röhricht Multimedia Point. 66877 Ramstein, Germany

(Second Edition), 2019

THE POWER OF INTERCESSION

STUDY GUIDE

Be diligent to present yourself approved to
God, a worker who does not need
to be ashamed, rightly dividing
the word of truth.

2 Timothy 2:15, NKJ

YINKA OLOYEDE

GLORY PUBLISHERS

AND RESOURCE SERVICES

Publishing and Teaching God's Word of Power

THIS STUDY GUIDE BELONGS TO:

____

MY SOCIAL MEDIA PLATFORMS ARE:

1 ______________________________________

2 ______________________________________

PHONE No

____

EMAIL

____

THIS STUDY GUIDE WAS WRITTEN

BY THE INSPIRATION

OF THE HOLY SPIRIT

A Call to Priesthood
in the Kingdom of our Lord

But you are a chosen generation,

a royal priesthood, a holy nation,

His own special people,

that you may proclaim the praises of Him

who called you out of darkness

into His marvelous light;

(1Peter 2:9)

FORWARD

My first contact with Pastor (Mrs.) Yinka Oloyede was a few months ago when she came from Germany in response to an invitation by the Intercessory Department of my church. Before then, members had spent months updating their knowledge of intercession using the book titled, The Power of Intercession, together with the study guide (which Pastor Yinka Oloyede authored). Her visit was to climax activities and round up the training. From these experiences, I discovered that Pastor (Mrs.) Oloyede is blessed with great spiritual impartation for her generation.

Her approach to intercession as detailed in the book and her brilliant presentation during her visit, assured me that she is one of the few servants that God has sent to the world to sharpen His children's knowledge of how to access His throne of grace, for prayers to be answered and to receive the spirit of discernment.

Also, through the introduction of her new work titled "God speaks to the unknown Prayer Journal." An innovative manner of approaching God through prayers has been revealed. The scriptures say that "For the revelation awaits an appointed time; it speaks of the end and will not prove false. Though it lingers, wait for it; it will certainly come and will not delay." (Habakkuk 2:3). Revelations or visions revealed in any form may and sometimes may not manifest immediately. It is beneficial to record them in the manner, recommended in this book so that no one will share the glory with our father in heaven.

A great work by a great servant of God. I recommend it for use.

Tony Dosumu
Fountain of Grace Ministries,
The United Kingdom.

AIMS OF THIS STUDY GUIDE

The aims of this study guidebook are designed to help those who would like to be more effective in their prayer life. It will help all intercessors to be more effective in their calling and encourage all those who would like to answer the call.

It is more helpful if you first read the book on the power of intercession before you go through this study guide. It will give you a basic biblical foundation on Intercession and Worship.

After studying both books, these are some of the principles you will learn:

- The difference between a praying believer and an intercessor.
- The importance of intercession in the world we live in today.
- How you can become an effective intercessor.
- Characteristics of an Intercessor.

- How you can become an active, genuine worshipper that God is looking for.
- How the power of praise will defeat your enemy.
- Importance of UNITY in the dress code of God.
- The positive effects of Fasting with the right attitude.
- How to be a productive citizen in the kingdom of God.
- The differences between the kingdom of light and the kingdom of darkness.
- Why We Must Go beyond the scope of Intercession.

Understanding the Written Layout of this Study Guide

Each chapter has questions to be answered in different ways; some might be explaining answers in your own words. I believe when a person can explain scriptures in his/her own words, they have a better understanding of what that scripture is saying, than just memorising it. When scriptures are not understood correctly, we misuse them, and therefore, we do not have the results we were expecting. Some questions are also just filling in the blanks and even other approaches.

Some of the chapters have practical exercises, which are assignments to test your ability on the new things you have learnt.

(2 Timothy 2:15)

15 Be diligent to present yourself approved to God, a worker who does not need to be ashamed, rightly dividing the word of truth.

You must do your best to answer all the test papers, so you can be sure you have fully understood what you have learnt (rightly dividing the word of truth). This will give you the confidence to put into practice what knowledge you have gained and also give you an opportunity to teach others.

Furthermore, there is a bonus explanatory of some other topics; for example, the study on spiritual War was explained from a different perspective to what we usually are acquainted with.

Another topic explained is, differentiating between the kingdom of God and the kingdom of Satan as well as their methods of winning people into their domain.

Conclusion

After one month of studying both books, you should certainly see a drastic change in your prayer life.

Note: If you have studied both books, done all the Test papers and practical exercises, and there is no change or improvement in any of the areas in your prayer life discussed in these books, we would like you to write or send us an email and let us know your area or areas of difficulty.

Email:

contact@glorypublishersworldwide.com

Table of Contents

Chapter One

WHO IS AN INTERCESSOR?

Test paper 1

1. After reading the book, can you distinguish between a praying believer and an intercessor?

i. What are the main concerns of a believer when praying?

____

____

____

____

____

ii. What are the main concerns of an intercessor when praying?

2. Read 1 Timothy 2:1-4 and explain in your own words, why it is necessary to pray for all kinds of leadership.

3. In your own words, what do you think Intercession is all about?

4a. What separates man from God? Read Isaiah 59:1-2.

____

____

____

____

____

____

4b. What is the root cause of your answer to question 4a?

____

____

____

____

____

____

5a. Is it possible that an un-confessed sin in your life can cause sickness?

Yes.... No....

5b. What does James 5:16 say about confession?

____

____

____

____

____

5c. What is James 5:16 saying about the prayers of a righteous man?

____

____

____

____

____

6. How does Noah's righteousness affect you today as a human being? (Genesis chapter 6)

____

____

____

____

____

7. How can you be like Noah and reconcile others to God? (**Hint**: Study what kind of relationship Noah had with God).

____

____

____

____

____

____

An Overview of this Chapter

This chapter is to give you a view of who is an intercessor and how your relationship with God can be useful in the earth realm.

Practical Exercise 1

1. Write out James 5:16 in different Bible versions and study them to remind yourself how powerful your prayers can be when you live right before God.

1. James 5:16, ... Bible.

2. James 5: 16.......................Bible.

2. Now explain James 5:16 in your own words and write out a prayer to guide you to have an effective prayer life.

Explanation:

Prayer guide:

Chapter Two

IMPORTANCE OF INTERCESSION

Test paper 2

1. Read the book of Numbers 16:47- 48 and explain the effect of Aaron's obedience to make atonement for the people.

____

____

____

____

____

____

2. Study the passage carefully and answer the following questions.

(Ezekiel 22:24-31)

24 "Son of man, say to her: 'You are a land that is not cleansed or rained on in the day of indignation.'

25 "The conspiracy of her ***prophets*** *in her midst is like a roaring lion tearing the prey; they have devoured people; they have taken treasure and precious things; they have made many widows in her midst.*

26 "Her ***priests*** *have violated My law and profaned My holy things; they have not distinguished between the holy and unholy, nor have they made known the difference between the unclean and the clean; and they have hidden their eyes from My Sabbaths so that I am profaned among them.*

27 "Her ***princes*** *in her midst are like wolves tearing the prey, to shed blood, to destroy people, and to get dishonest gain.*

28 "Her ***prophets*** *plastered them with untempered mortar, seeing false visions, and divining lies for them, saying, 'Thus says the Lord GOD,' when the LORD had not spoken.*

29 "The ***people*** *of the land have used oppressions, committed robbery, and mistreated the poor and needy; and they wrongfully oppress the stranger.*

30 "So I sought for a man among them who would make a wall, and stand in the gap before Me on behalf of the land, that I should not destroy it; but I found no one.

31 "Therefore I have poured out My indignation on them; I have consumed them with the fire of My wrath; and I have recompensed their deeds on their own heads," says the Lord GOD.

Questions:

2a. Name the categories of people God was addressing in this passage.

1. ______________________________

____

2. ______________________________

____

3. ______________________________

____

4. ______________________________

____

2b. What were the accusations that God pointed out to each group? State at least three for each group.

Group1: ______________________________

i. ______________________________

____

ii. ______________________________

____

iii. ______________________________________

____

Group2: ______________________________

i. ______________________________________

____

ii. ______________________________________

____

iii. ______________________________________

____

Group3: ______________________________

i. ______________________________________

____

ii. ______________________________________

____

iii. ______________________________________

____

Group 4: ______________________________

i. ______________________________________

____

ii. ______________________________________

____

iii. ______________________________________

____

3. Why did God have to destroy the land?

____

____

____

____

____

____

____

4. Explain in your own words, Ezekiel 22:30.

____

____

____

____

____

____

____

____

5. Relating your answers to questions 1-4; why did Paul admonish (warn about) that we should pray for people in authority? 1 Timothy 2:1-4.

____

____

____

____

____

____

An Overview of this Chapter

From studying both cases, the importance of intercession must have been made clear enough and why we must pray for people in authority. It might be government authority, people in church leadership or your working environment.

Practical Exercise 2

Write two prayer points each for the following leadership authority that you know.

- Church leadership.

- Government leadership.
- Work leadership.
- Home leadership.
- School leadership.

How to record your prayer points

Identify the problems in each leadership, and use that as a guide for your prayer request.

NB: Sometimes general prayers are not effective as identifying the problem and then praying for the solution.

If you have no idea about the problems going on in any of the leaderships mentioned above, pray in the Holy Spirit.

Chapter Three

HOW TO PRAY EFFECTIVELY

Test paper 3

1. What is the difference between interceding and praying?

Interceding:

____

____

____

____

____

____

____

____

Praying:

____

____

____

____

____

____

2. Study this passage: 2 Chronicles 7:13-15.

We usually read this scripture when praying for repentance. In most cases, we start from verse 14, which is a continuation of verse 13, because it starts with an **"if."** The **"if"** is the MOST important part of this passage.

Below is verse 13 and 14 as a continuation of each other.

After studying this scripture, can you point out the importance of the **"if"** in the passage?

(2 Chronicles 7:13-14)

*"When I shut up heaven and there is no rain, or command the locusts to devour the land or send pestilence among My people, "**if** My*

people who are called by My name will humble themselves, and pray and seek My face, and turn from their wicked ways, then I will hear from heaven, and will forgive their sin and heal their land.

Answer:

____

____

____

____

____

____

3. In your own words, write out four conditions in which you can be rest assured that your prayers have been answered. (Hint: study Solomon's conversation with God after the dedication of the temple 2 Chronicles 7:14).

1. ____

____

2. ____

____

3. ____

____

4. ____

____

4. Read Colossians 2:9-10. Study its explanation using the Amplified Bible and answer the following questions.

Colossians 2:9-10, NKJV version.

For in Him the whole fullness of Deity (the Godhead) continues to dwell in bodily form [giving complete expression of the divine nature].

Colossians 2:9-10, Amplified Bible version.

And you are in Him, made full and having come to fullness of life [in Christ you too are filled with the Godhead, Father, Son and Holy Spirit-and reach full spiritual stature]. And He is the Head of all rule and authority [of every angelic principality and power].

Colossians 2:9-10, in the Amplified Bible, is explained with the following points:

1. God's divine full nature is in Christ in human form (God's divine nature is the Trinity; God the Father, God the Son, God the Holy Spirit or we can simply say the Godhead).

2. Since we are now a new person in Christ, we also have the Godhead living in us. (Read, Colossians 3:16).

3. Christ is the head over all rule and authority.

This passage is giving us the awareness of who we are in Christ. If we can really understand that we have the GODHEAD living in us, we should also know that we have the headship over all rule and authority in us (angelic principality and power). However, we must daily conform; strive towards righteous living, which is the nature of God, and is hidden in Christ. We can only become more Christ-like by practising the four conditions God gave

Solomon. Then we will be able to manifest the authority that is in us.

Questions:

4a. From the explanation given, what does it mean to have the GODHEAD living in you?

____

____

____

____

____

____

____

4b. In your own words, how can you express the authority of the GODHEAD living in you?

____

____

____

____

____

____

____

____

An Overview of this Chapter

The reader has a better perspective of how to pray effectively and the awareness of the authority of the Godhead in them.

Practical Prayer Exercise 3

Study Daniel, chapter 9, and note the prayer sequence. Using Daniel's sequence of prayer, form your own prayer sequence for a nation, you know. (Note: you must have some information about that nation to make your prayer request, or you pray in the Holy Spirit).

Prayer Sequence

1. Worship (Adoration and Thanksgiving)

____

____

____

____

____

____

____

____

2. Humbleness (Confession of sins)

3. Forgiveness (Ask for Forgiveness)

4. Supplication (Make your Prayer Request known).

Isaiah, 65:24, assures you that your prayers have been answered.

Isaiah 65:24

24 "It shall come to pass

That before they call, I will answer;

And while they are still speaking, I will hear.

5. Thanksgiving (Praise the Lord in Faith)

____

Chapter Four

THE KINGDOM OF LIGHT VERSUS THE KINGDOM OF DARKNESS

Test paper 4

1. Anytime you see a rainbow in the sky, how does it remind you about the love of God for mankind?

____

____

____

____

____

2. Read Mathew 24:6-14. Most of the time, when we talk about this passage our minds focus on the wars between different countries, but the real war is between the kingdom of light and the kingdom of darkness. Jesus is the king of the kingdom of light while Satan is the prince (not a king) of the kingdom of darkness. Each one has a means of winning people into their kingdom.

The kingdom of light

The Kingdom of light; Jesus is the head of the kingdom of light. All authority in heaven and on earth has been given to Jesus (Matthew 28:18). The whole Godhead is in Jesus and, He is the head over all rule and authority; in other words, overall angelic principality and power (Colossians 2:9-10).

Methods of winning people into His kingdom

1. God's sacrifice of His Son, Jesus Christ, to die for the whole world so that everyone will

have an opportunity to be saved from destruction in the kingdom of darkness (John 3:16).

2. Jesus has promised us abundant life in Him (John 10:10).

3. Jesus Christ is not in a hurry to come back but is waiting patiently that everyone will repent and come into His kingdom (2 Peter 3:9, Mathew 6:14).

4. Through our prayers of intercession and spreading the good news of salvation (2 Corinthians 5:18-21). Jesus Christ has given us the ministry of reconciliation to bring others into the awareness of His kingdom.

5. Through the power of the Holy Spirit to help us stay on the course of our Christian walk (John 16:7-8, Romans 8:5).

6. Through the Word of God, which teaches us the difference between good and evil (Hebrews 4:12).

The kingdom of darkness

Satan is the prince of the kingdom of darkness. The reason why Satan is a prince and not a king is because Christ has the rulership over all powers and authority in heaven and on earth. Satan was thrown out of heaven down to earth (Revelation 12:7-9) and has only a short time to exist before he is finally destroyed to burn in the lake of fire forever (Revelation 12:12, Revelation 20:10).

Methods of winning people into his kingdom

1. Through temptation, he lures us to do his will and go against God (Matthew 4:3).

2. Through deception: he deceives us to go against God's instruction (Genesis 3:1-6).

3. Through lies (John 8:44).

4. Through destruction (John 10:10).

5. By veiling the unbeliever to the word of the gospel to prevent the glory of God from shining on them (2 Corinthians 4:3-4).

6. By rebelling against God (Revelation 12:9).

Jesus gives a distinction between these two kingdoms

(Matthew 12:25-30)

25 But Jesus knew their thoughts and said to them: "Every kingdom divided against itself is brought to desolation, and every city or house divided against itself will not stand.

26 "If Satan casts out Satan, he is divided against himself. How then will his kingdom stand?

28 "But if I cast out demons by the Spirit of God, surely the kingdom of God has come upon you.

29 "Or how can one enter a strong man's house and plunder his goods, unless he first binds the strong man? And then he will plunder his house.

30 "He who is not with Me is against Me, and he who does not gather with Me scatters abroad.

Matthew 12: 30 in THE Message Bible, state's it this way:

"This is war, and there is no neutral ground. If you're not on my side, you're the enemy; if you're not helping, you're making things worse."

Explanation of Matthew 12:25-30

In this passage, Jesus is distinguishing between the kingdom of God, which is the kingdom of light, and the kingdom of Satan, which is the kingdom of darkness.

Demons are agents of Satan; therefore, Jesus casting out demons from the people God created is a sign to Satan that the kingdom of God has come to wage war against his kingdom in the life of the people.

Jesus death on the cross of Calvary and his resurrection on the third day is the evidence or proof that Jesus has the ultimate victory over Satan. Since Satan has been defeated, Jesus has the power to destroy all the demonic agents of Satan. He, therefore, also has the power to destroy his works of perversion. Perversion means turning from the true purpose or refusing to do right; Jesus says you are healed, but Satan says you are sick. Others are poverty, diseases, demonic bondage, and veiling people to hear the gospel which is people being defiant to the preaching of the gospel.

Destroying one's destiny in life by captivating people in their minds to be in demonic bondage, will lead them to live a life with no hope or no future regretting they were ever born. All the works of Satan are a perversion of what Jesus has truly said about us.

But Jesus came preaching the good news of the kingdom of God to set us free from every attack that comes against us from the kingdom of Satan; He has come to give us life and give it in abundance.

Since we know the distinction between both kingdoms, there is no in-between or neutral ground; it is either good or evil. The Message Bible calls it a **war** and Jesus said, "If you are not on His side, you are on the enemy's side." Jesus has now given us the obligation to preach the gospel of the kingdom of God to win more people to His side.

The Great Commission (Mark 16:15-20)

15 And He said to them, "Go into all the world and preach the gospel to every creature.

16 "He who believes and is baptized will be saved, but he who does not believe will be condemned.

17 "And these signs will follow those who believe: In My name they will cast out demons; they will speak with new tongues;

18 "they will take up serpents; and if they drink anything deadly, it will by no means hurt them; they will lay hands on the sick, and they will recover."

19 So then, after the Lord had spoken to them, He was received up into heaven, and sat down at the right hand of God.

20 And they went out and preached everywhere, the Lord working with them and confirming the word through the accompanying signs. Amen.

Jesus is giving us the same instructions that He gave His disciples and He promised to be working with us. Our obedience to our calling is a sign that we are on the Lord's side in this war. Jesus also said that "since the days of John the Baptist until now the kingdom of heaven suffers violence, and the violent take it by force (Matthew 11:12)."

Violent means to be aggressive; we have to be aggressive in our calling to advance the kingdom.

Ask yourself this question today:

WHO'S SIDE DO YOU BELONG TO?

Questions:

2a. Mention two methods Jesus uses to win people into His kingdom.

1. ______________________________

____

2. ____

____

2b. Mention two methods Satan uses to win people into his kingdom.

1. ____

____

2. ____

____

2c. From the above explanation, give at least four differences between the products of the kingdom of light and the works of perversion from the kingdom of darkness. (You can give other examples that were not mentioned in the above passage).

Kingdom of Light	Kingdom of Darkness

Kingdom of Light	Kingdom of Darkness

2d. What is the effect of your prayers of intercession on the kingdom of darkness?

____

____

____

____

____

3. What was the effect of Abraham's prayer of intercession on Sodom and Gomorrah?

____

____

____

____

____

An Overview of this Chapter

This chapter explains the precise difference between the kingdom of light and the kingdom of darkness. God needed Abraham to intercede for Lot and all his relations to save them from destruction, so also does He need us to intercede for unbelievers so that, their life might be saved from destruction.

Practical exercise 4

What other identities do you think you are holding that belong to the kingdom of darkness and you need to get rid of.

1. Write at least four of them down.
2. Find scriptures about each identity.
3. Pray with the scriptures each day until you see a change.
4. Make sure you remind yourself of what the scripture says about you in that area each time it shows up.

NB: You must listen **to the voice** of the **Holy Spirit**, who will help you to live out your new identity by being **obedient** to Him and **not ignoring His correction**.

Chapter Five

RELATING YOUR CHARACTER TO THE EFFECTIVENESS OF YOUR PRAYERS

Test paper 5

1. Give three reasons why Job had a meaningful relationship with God?

____

____

____

____

____

____

2. How would you explain the attitude of Job's friends? (Job 42:7)

____

____

____

____

____

____

3. Explain in your own words, Job 42:8.

____

____

____

____

____

____

Fill in the blanks

4a. Job's obedience was a form of

____

____

____

____

4b His obedience to pray over their sacrifice proved his to his friends.

4c. God answered his prayers and restored Job because he his friends.

5. What lesson can we learn from Job, as an intercessor?

6. Give one similarity between Moses and Jesus?

____

____

____

____

____

____

7. Give two similarities between a priest and an intercessor?

1. ____

____

____

2. ____

____

____

8. Explain 1 Peter 2:9-10 in your own words.

____

____

____

____

9. What was the effect of Jesus intercession for Peter? (Luke 22:31-32)

1. ____

____

____

2. ____

____

____

3. ____

____

____

10. State 4 prayer points of Jesus' intercession to the Father.

1. ____

____

____

2. ____

____

____

3. ______________________________________

____

____

4. ______________________________________

____

____

11. State two effects of the Holy Spirit's intercession through us.

1. ______________________________________

____

____

2. ______________________________________

____

____

An Overview of this Chapter

This chapter points out the importance of our prayers of intercession and how our character relates to the effectiveness of our prayers.

We are called to be a royal priesthood in action through our lifestyle of worship and interceding on behalf of unbelievers.

We should also be confident in our calling, knowing that Jesus is interceding for us in heaven, and we also have the Holy Spirit to make intercession for us according to the will of God.

Chapter Six

THE IMPORTANCE OF RELEASING GOD'S POWER THROUGH PRAYER

Test paper 6

1. What was the importance of Jesus asking His disciples to wait in the upper room in Jerusalem?

____

____

____

____

____

2. As a child of God, what advantage do you have over people in the Old Testament?

____

____

____

____

____

____

3. How was Elijah able to demonstrate the power of prayer to Israel?

____

____

____

____

____

____

4. King Pharaoh asked Moses to intercede for him. Moses interceded for Pharaoh, and God answered his prayers (Exodus 8: 8-13 & 28-31). What does this imply to you when you pray for other people or nations that do not know God?

5. Is it possible to release God's power without being baptised in the Holy Spirit?

Yes.......... ..... No...............

Explain in your own words.

An Overview of this Chapter

We need the Holy Spirit to release the power of God through us.

We also have the power to intercede for unbelievers or other nations that do not know God.

Chapter Seven

WORSHIP

Test paper 7

1. Define the term **"worship"** in your own words?

____

____

____

____

____

____

2. How can you express true reverence to God? (Read 2 Corinthians 7:1 & 1 Peter 1:17).

____

____

____

____

____

____

3. What is the difference between Adoration and Thanksgiving?

____

____

____

____

____

____

4. Job, Jehoshaphat, Paul and Silas were examples of people who praised the Lord in faith. Choosing any of these examples mentioned, explain in your own words how they praised the Lord in faith, and what was the result of their action?

4a. Explanation:

____

____

____

____

____

____

4b. The Result:

____

____

____

____

____

____

5. Why is Revelation 12:11, significant to identify your victory over your situation?

____

____

____

____

____

____

6. Meditate on Yinka's phrase and write out your own phrase in your own words.

____

____

____

____

____

____

(.......................................,.....)

(NAME, YEAR)

7. Our devotional worship of God is said to be our spiritual act of worship and our truthful act of worship. Explain both.

7a____

____

____

____

7b____

____

____

____

8. Give three differences between a genuine worshipper and a worshipper.

(Read James 1: 22-25)

Genuine Worshipper	Worshipper

9. Give examples of 4 elements of worship and the importance of each one.

1. ______________________________

____

2. ______________________________

____

3. ______________________________

____

4. ____

____

10. In chapter five of the book, it is evident that the priests played a vital role in worship. How can worship be a significant role in your life as an Intercessor?

____

____

____

____

____

____

____

11. How can you help to reconcile sinners to God?

____

____

____

____

____

____

____

12. How did David develop an intimate relationship with God?

____

____

____

____

____

____

____

____

____

13. How can you improve your relationship with God?

____

____

____

____

____

____

____

____

____

14. What areas of your life do you need to improve to become a genuine worshipper that the Lord is seeking and not just a worshipper?

____

____

____

____

____

____

An Overview of this Chapter

This chapter explains in detail the meaning of worship and who is a genuine worshipper. It also describes the importance of expressing worship.

Practical Exercise 5

1. Write out five names of God and their meaning. Use them daily to start your prayer time by adoring Him. Read a Psalm at least three times a week.

1. ______________________________

____

____

2. ______________________________

____

____

3. ______________________________

____

____

4. ______________________________

____

____

5. ______________________________

____

____

Do this consecutively for one month.

After practising this for a month, write down five ways how this has improved your prayer life.

1. ____

____

____

2. ____

____

____

3. ____

____

____

4. ____

____

____

5. ____

____

____

Has your lifestyle of worship improved?

Yes……No……

How/ why?

____

____

____

____

____

____

Note: if your lifestyle of worship has not improved, study the chapter in the book again, but at a slower pace. If you have any questions, email us at info@glorypublishers.org

Chapter Eight

COOPERATE INTERCESSION

Test paper 8

1. It was evident in John chapter 17 that Jesus was passionate about Unity amongst all believers. Summarise, in your own words the reason why.

____

____

____

____

____

____

2. Jesus taught His disciples about the importance of agreement in prayer. Explain this scripture in your own words, using any Bible version of your choice.

(Matthew 18:18-20) ……………….Bible

____

____

____

____

____

____

____

3. Why is it essential for you as an intercessor to be in unity with others in prayer? (Hint: read Leviticus 26:8).

____

____

____

____

____

____

____

4. Explain this sentence:

"Where there is unity, God commands His blessing." (Psalm 133)

____

____

____

____

____

____

____

____

5a. What was the effect of the believers' constant prayer for Peter while he was in prison? (Acts 12:5-17)

____

____

____

____

____

____

____

____

Using Acts 12:5-17, fill in the blanks below:

6a. While the believers were still praying for Peter, God answered, this was a

____

6b. How can you be part of a

____

(Hint: Your answer in 6a)

____

____

____

____

____

____

6c. We see a lot of miracles happening at large conferences because people go

____

____

____

____

7. We must release

____

within us through

____

And

____

to do His

____

An Overview of this Chapter

This chapter exemplifies Jesus Spirit of unity for the church and its benefits. It also gives examples of the effects of cooperate prayer.

FASTING

Study chapter 6 in the book very carefully before you answer the questions.

Test paper 9

---

1. In a simple sentence, define fasting in your own words.

____

____

____

____

____

____

____

2. How do you feed the soul-man?

____

____

____

____

____

____

3. How do you feed the spirit-man?

____

____

____

____

____

____

4. What is the product of your soul-man?

____

____

____

____

____

____

____

5. What is the product of your spirit-man?

____

____

____

____

____

____

6. What are the 7 Benefits of fasting?

1. ______________________________________

____

____

2. ______________________________________

____

____

3. ______________________________________

____

____

4. ______________________________________

____

____

5. ______________________________________

____

____

6. ______________________________________

____

____

6. ______________________________________

____

____

7. Describe cooperate fasting in your own words.

____

____

____

____

____

____

8. From the examples of cooperate fasting in the book, we observed that their first step in handling any situation was to go on a fast. Out

of the six examples given in the book, state one effect of each from any five of them.

1. ______________________________

____

____

2. ______________________________

____

____

3. ______________________________

____

____

4. ______________________________

____

____

5. ______________________________

____

____

9. Why couldn't the disciples cast out the death and dumb spirit? (Mark 9:17-29)

____

____

____

____

____

____

10. What did the disciples need to cast out the death and dumb spirit?

____

____

____

____

____

11. How did Jesus say they could get it? And quote the scripture.

____

____

____

____

____

12. Out of the seven points given in the book why cooperate fasting is important, state two of them in your own words or how you understood them.

1. ____

____

____

2. ____

____

____

13. Why is fasting important to you as an individual?

____

____

____

____

____

____

____

____

____

____

An Overview of this Chapter

Sometimes people go on a hunger strike, and they call it a fast; however, this chapter gives a detailed definition of fasting. It also explains how and why we need to fast.

It is also essential that the outcome of fasting must always be evident to the individual or the cooperate group.

Chapter Ten

THE KINGDOM OF GOD

Test paper 10

War is defined as an armed conflict between two (group of state) states; state of opposition or hostility; the profession of arms.

Armed; means to carry weapons.

A warrior is a fighting man or a brave soldier.

Warfare also means fighting.

1. Bearing in mind the above definitions, give three differences between Spiritual warfare and Worldly warfare.

Spiritual Warfare	Worldly Warfare

2. Give three reasons why it is important as an intercessor to be baptised in the Holy Spirit with the evidence of speaking in tongues.

1. ____________________________________

____

____

2. ____________________________________

____

____

3. ______________________________

____

____

3. Explain three qualities of a spiritual soldier, and quote Scriptures for each point.

1. Scripture:

____

____

____

____

____

____

____

Scripture:

____

____

____

____

____

____

____

Scripture:

4. What does this scripture mean to you? Romans 11:29

5. Explain in your own words, how God has assured and empowered your calling? (Read 2 Peter 1:3-11) Use any Bible version to explain your answer.

The kingdom of God versus the kingdom of Satan

We defined the kingdom of God, as God's rule of grace (underserved merit) in the world or in a believer who allows Jesus to be Lord of their life.

We can therefore say,

The kingdom of Satan is Satan's rule of grace-lessness (deserved disadvantage, weakness, difficulty, and drawback) in the life of a person (believer or unbeliever) who allows Satan and his demonic entourage to be lord of their life.

(Yinka Oloyede, 2007)

Romans 14:17 says that for the Kingdom of God is ***not*** *eating and drinking, but righteousness and peace and joy in the Holy Spirit.*

We can also say that,

The kingdom of Satan **is** eating and drinking and also includes unrighteousness (wickedness, ungodliness) and war and sorrow in demonic spirits.

(Yinka Oloyede, 2007)

6. Explain in your own words, what is the kingdom of Satan?

____

____

____

____

____

____

(......................,...............)

Name Year

7. Explain in your own words, what is the kingdom of God?

____

____

____

____

____

____

(..........................,..............)

Name Year

9. List the Nine Fruit of the Spirit from Galatians 6:22-23.

1. ______________________________

2. ______________________________

3. ______________________________

4. ______________________________

5. ______________________________

6. ______________________________

7. ______________________________

8. ______________________________

9. ______________________________

10. What does the nine fruit of the Spirit represent?

____

____

____

____

____

____

11. How can we attract unbelievers to be part of God's kingdom?

____

____

____

____

____

____

12. *Colossians 1:13 say's that God has delivered us from the power of darkness and conveyed us into the kingdom of the Son of His love.*

Therefore, we are now citizens of the kingdom of God.

Give four areas of your life that used to identify your old citizenship and four areas of your life that you surely know you have changed your identity.

Old Identity	New Identity

13. What does it mean to be an Ambassador of Christ? (2 Corinthians 5:18)

14. Give a summary of what you have learned in this chapter.

____

____

____

____

An Overview of this Chapter

This chapter will allow the reader to know the distinct difference between the kingdom of God and the kingdom of Satan. We must understand that we are at ***war*** *with the kingdom of darkness if we claim to be on the Lord's side.*

Satan is in opposition to God's kingdom; as a result, we are God's agents fighting Satan's kingdom by our obedience to our calling (chapter seven).

We also must be sure to know whose identity we are flashing to the world.

Both kingdoms are in this world, which one of them are you operating from?
(Something to ponder on)

Chapter Eleven

GOING BEYOND THE SCOPE OF INTERCESSION

Test paper 12

1. What are the three key factors in the life of an intercessor?

1. ____

____

____

2. ____

____

____

3. ____

____

____

2. Give examples of three people who prayed to God for a specific situation. What actions did they have to carry out to accomplish the mission and see the result of their prayer? Write out one action or step in each case.

1. ____

____

____

2. ____

____

____

3. ____

____

____

3. Reading the book and going through this study guide, what is your new perspective or view about intercession and an intercessor?

Give a 2-point summary.

1. ____

____

____

2. ____

____

____

4. How has this book inspired you to become more effective in your prayer life?

____

____

____

____

____

____

5. Give a general overview of this chapter.

____

____

____

____

____

6. Give a general overview of the Power of Intercession study guide book.

____

____

____

____

____

____

7. What areas of this book did you not fully comprehend?

____

____

____

____

____

Click on the link below if you have any questions.

https://glorypublishers.org/contact/

or write to us at

contact@glorypublishers.org

8. Would you recommend this book to other people?

Yes.................... No......................

9. Explain three reasons for your answer to question 8.

1. ____

____

2. ____

____

3. ____

____

10. What grade would you award the author of this book? Pick the grade of your choice.

A. EXCELLENT

B. VERY GOOD

C. GOOD

D. AVERAGE

E. BELOW AVERAGE

F. FAILURE

NEXT STEP

Now that you have understood what it means to be an Intercessor by studying both the Power of Intercession and the Power of Intercession Study guide, you have prepared yourself to start writing in your Intercessory Prayer Journal.

Keeping a Prayer Journal for your time of Intercession is the key to helping you grow and mature as an Intercessor. It will also help you to hear and understand the instructions of the Holy Spirit as you write daily in your Prayer Journal.

A FREE GIFT FOR YOU

THE INTERCESSORY PRAYER JOURNAL

God's Vision note For Me; is to guide you in praying the heartbeat of God and manifesting His Will on earth as you begin your prayer journaling journey.

If you follow the guidelines given in the first few pages of this journal notebook, your life as an intercessor will become more productive and effective.

Click on the link to get your free gift

http://getbook.at/IntercessionJournal

Thank you for studying the Power of Intercession Study guide. We would like you to take the next step and write a review of this book on Amazon and/or our website.

In His Service,

Yinka Oloyede

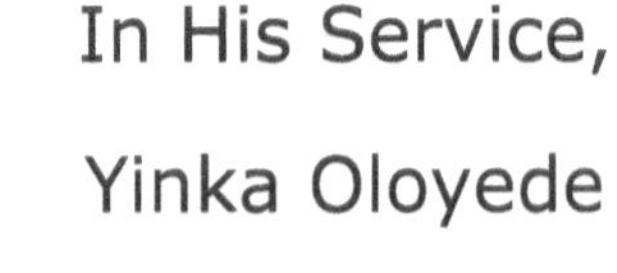

CLICK HERE TO WRITE A REVIEW

OR EMAIL US

Email: contact@glorypublishersworldwide.com

Thank you.

CONTACT DETAILS OF

YINKA OLOYEDE

Website: www.glorypublishersworldwide.com

Email: contact@glorypublishersworld-wide.com

Tel: +49 (0) 17687017796

Link to her books on Amazon

amazon http://viewauthor.at/GloryPublishersBooks

https://www.instagram.com/glorypublishers2/

https://www.youtube.com/@glory-publishersworldwide

Publishing and Teaching God's Word of Power.

www.ingramcontent.com/pod-product-compliance
Lightning Source LLC
LaVergne TN
LVHW091330190726
843491LV00002B/644

9783944924229